Mrs. Budlong's Christmas Presents

RUPERT HUGHES

[ZHINGOORA BOOKS]

This edition is published by
Zhingoora Books.

The Cover is Designed by Pallav Sethiya.

CONTENTS

MRS. BUDLONG'S CHRISTMAS PRESENTS

I

AT THE SIGN OF THE PIANO LAMP

The morning after Christmas Eve is the worst morning-after there is. The very house suffers the headache that follows a prolonged spree. Remorse stalks at large; remorse for the things one gave—and did not give—and got.

Everybody must act a general glee which can be felt only specifically, if at all. Everybody must exclaim about everything Oh! and Ah! and How Sweet of You! and Isn't it Perfectly Dear! The very THING I Wanted! and How DID you EVER Guess it?

Christmas morning in the town of Carthage is a day when most of the people keep close at home, for Christmas is another passover. It is Santa Claus that passes over.

People in Carthage are not rich; the shops are not grandiose, and inter-family presents are apt to be trivial and futile—or worse yet, utile.

The Carthaginian mother generally finds that Father has credited the hat she got last fall, to this Christmas; the elder brothers receive warm under-things and the young ones brass-toed boots, mitts and mufflers. The girls may find something ornamental in their stockings, and their stockings may be silk or nearly—but then girls have to be foolishly diked up anyway, or they will never be married out. Dressing up daughters comes under the head of window-display or coupons, and is charged off to publicity.

Nearly everybody in Carthage—except Mrs. Ulysses S. G. Budlong—celebrates Christmas behind closed doors. People find it easier to rhapsodize when the collateral is not shown. It is amazing how far a Carthaginian can go on the most meager donation. The formula is usually: "We had such a lovely Christmas at our house. What did I get? Oh, so many things I can't remember!"

But Mrs. Ulysses S. G. Budlong does not celebrate her Christmasses behind closed doors—or rather she did not: a strange change came over her this last Christmas. She used to open her doors wide—metaphorically, that is; for there was a storm-door with a spring on it to keep the cold draught out of the hall.

As regular as Christmas itself was the oh-quite-informal reception Mrs. Budlong gave to mitigate the ineffable stupidity of Christmas afternoon: that dolorous period when one meditates the ancient platitude that anticipation is better than realization; and suddenly understands why it is blesseder to give than to receive: because one does not have to wear what one gives away.

On Christmas Mrs. U. S. G. Budlong took all the gifts she had gleaned, and piled them on and around the baby grand piano in the back parlor. There was a piano lamp there, one of those illuminated umbrellas—about as large and as useful as a date-palm tree.

Along about that time in the afternoon when the Christmas dinner becomes a matter of hopeless remorse, Mrs. Budlong's neighbors were expected to drop in and view the loot under the lamp. It looked like hospitality, but it felt like hostility. She passed her neighbors under the yoke and gloated over her guests, while seeming to overgloat her gifts.

But she got the gifts. There was no question of that. By hook or by crook she saw to it that the bazaar under the piano lamp always groaned.

One of the chief engines for keeping up the display was the display itself. Everybody who knew Mrs. Budlong—and not to know Mrs. Budlong was to argue oneself unknown—knew that he or she would be invited to this Christmas triumph. And being invited rather implied being represented in the tribute.

Hence ensued a curious rivalry in Carthage. People vied with each other in giving Mrs. Budlong presents; not that they loved Mrs. Budlong more, but that they loved comparisons less.

The rivalry had grown to ridiculous proportions. But of course Mrs. Budlong did not care how ridiculous it grew; for it could hardly have escaped her shrewd eyes how largely it advantaged her that people should give her presents in order to show other people that some people needn't think they could show off before other people without having other people show that they could show off, too, as well as other people could. The pyschology must be correct, for it is incoherent.

Mrs. Budlong herself was never known to break any of the commandments, but in her back parlor her neighbors made flitters of the one against coveting thy neighbor's and-so-forth and so-on.

It was when Mr. and Mrs. County Road Supervisor Detwiller were walking home from one of these occasions, that Mr. Detwiller was saying: "Well, ain't Mizzes Budlong the niftiest little gift-getter that ever held up a train? How on earth did we happen to get stung?"

"I don't know, Roscoe. It's one of those things you can't get out of without getting out of town too. Here we've been and gone and skimped our own children to buy something that would show up good in Mrs. Budlong's back parlor, and when I laid eyes on it in all that clutter—why, if it didn't look like something the cat brought in, I'll eat it!"

Mr. Detwiller had only one consolation—and he grinned over it:

"Well, there's no use cryin' over spilt gifts. But did you see how she stuck old Widower Clute for that Japanese porcelain vace—I notice she called it vahs?"

"Porcelain?" sniffed Mrs. Detwiller. "Paper musshay!"

"Well, getting even a paper—what you said—from old Clute is equal to extracting solid gold from anybody else. He's the stingiest man in sev'n states. He don't care any more for a two dollar bill than he does for his right eye. I bet she gave him ether before he let go."

"Oh, she works all the old bachelors and widowers that way," said Mrs. Detwiller, with a mixture of contempt and awe. "Invites 'em to a dinner party or two around Christmas marketing time, and begins to talk about how pretty the shops are and how tempting everything she wants is; says she saw a nimitation bronze clock at Strouther and Streckfuss's that it almost broke her heart to leave there. But o' course she couldn't afford to buy those kind of things for herself now when she's got to remember all her dear friends, and she runs on and on and the old batch growls, 'Stung again!' and goes to Strouther and Streckfuss's and tells Mr. Streckfuss to send Mrs. Budlong that blamed bronze clock she was admiring. And that's how she gets things. I could do it myself if I'd a mind to."

Mr. Detwiller felt that there was more envy than truth in this last remark, and he was rash enough to speak up for justice: "You could if you'd a mind to? Yep. If you'd a mind to! That's what somebody said about Shakespeare's plays. 'I could a wrote 'em myself if I'd a mind to,' says he, and somebody else said, 'Yes, if you'd a mind to,' he says. And that's about it. Any body could do what Mizzes Budlong does if they had the mind to; but the thing is, she's got the mind to. She goes after the gifts—and gits 'em. She don't almost git 'em, and she ain't goin' to git 'em. She gits 'em. And what gits me is how she gits 'em."

"Roscoe Detwiller, if you're goin' to praise that woman in the presence of your own lawful wife, I'll never speak to you the longest day I live." "Who's praisin' her? I was just sayin'—"

"Why, Roscoe Detwiller, you did, too! And I should think you'd be ashamed of yourself."

"Say, what ails you? Why, I was roastin' her to beat the band."

"And to think that on Christmas day of all days I should live to hear my own husband that I've loved and cherished and worked my fingers to the bone and never got any thanks and other women keepin' two and three hired girls, and after him denyin' his own children things to get expensive presents for a shameless creature like that Budlong woman—"

All over Carthage on Christmas afternoons couples were similarly at loggerheads over Mrs. Budlong's annual triumph.

Now of course Mrs. Budlong did not get all those presents without giving presents. Not in Carthage! It might have been possible to bamboozle these people one Christmas, but never another. Mrs. Budlong gave heaps of presents. Christmas was an industry with her, an ambition; Christmas was her career. It had long ago lost its religious significance for her, as for nearly everybody else in Carthage. Even Mr. Frankenstein (the Pantatorium magnate) is one of the most ardent advertisers of Christmas bargains, while Isidore Strouther and Esau Streckfuss are "almost persuaded" every December. They might be entirely persuaded if it were not for the scenes they witness in their aisles during the last weeks of Yuletide and the aftermath of trying to collect from the Gentile husbands during Billtide.

Mrs. Budlong's Christmas presents were of two sorts: those she made herself and those she made her husband pay for. He was the typical husband who never fails to settle his wife's bills, so long as he may raise a row about them till his wife cries and looks like an expensive luxury which only a really successful man could afford. Then he subsides until the first of the next month.

II

CHRONICLES OF A CRAFTSMAN

Mrs. Budlong's campaign was undertaken with the same farsightedness as a magazine editor's. On or about the Fourth of July she began to worry and plan. By the second week in August she had her tatting well under way. By the middle of September she was getting in her embroidered doilies. The earliest frost rarely surprised her with her quilts untufted. And when the first snow flew, her sachet bags were all stuffed and smelly.

She was very feminine in her sense of the value of her own time. At missionary meetings she would shed tears over the pathetic pictures of Oriental women who spent a year weaving a rug which would sell for a paltry hundred dollars and last a mere century or two. Then she would cheerfully devote fifteen days of incessant stitching at something she carried round in a sort of drumhead. At the end of that time she would have completed a more or less intolerable piece of colored fabric which she called a "drape" or a "throw." It could not be duplicated at a shop for less than $1.75, and it would wash perhaps three times.

Mr. Budlong once figured that if sweat-shop proprietors paid wages at the scale Mrs. Budlong established for herself, all the seamstresses and seamsters would curl up round their machines and die of starvation the first week. But he never told Mrs. Budlong this. Fancy stitching did not earn much, but it did not cost much; and it kept her mysteriously contented. She was stitching herself to her own home all the time.

The Christmas presents Mrs. Budlong made herself were not all a matter of needle and thread. Not at all! One year she turned her sewing room into a smithy. She gave Mr. and Mrs. Doctor Tisnower the loveliest hand-hammered brass coal scuttle that ever was seen.—and with a purple ribbon

10

tied to its tail. They kept flowers in it several summers, till one cruel winter a new servant put coal in it and completely scuttled it.

The same year she gave Mrs. ex-Mayor Cinnamon a hammered brass version of a C. D. Gibson drawing. The lady and gentleman looked as if they had broken out with a combination of yellow fever and smallpox, or suffered from enlarged pores or something. And the plum-colored plush frame didn't sit very well on the vermilion wall paper. But Mrs. Cinnamon hung it over the sofa in the expectation of changing the paper some day. It stayed there until the fateful evening when Mr. Nelson Chur called on Miss Editha Cinnamon and was just warming up a proposal that had held over almost as long as the wall paper, when bang! down came the overhanging brass drawing and bent itself hopelessly on Mr. Chur's skull. Mr. Chur said something that may have been Damocles. But he did not propose, and Mrs. Budlong was weeks wondering why Mrs. Cinnamon was so snippy to her.

The hammered brass era gave way to the opposite extreme of painted velvet. They say it is a difficult art; and it may well be. Mrs. Budlong's first landscape might as well have been painted on the side of her Scotch collie.

Her most finished roses had something of the look of shaggy tarantulas that had fallen into a paint pot and emerged in a towering rage. It was in that velvetolene stratum that she painted for the church a tasseled pulpit cloth that hung down a yard below the Bible. Dr. Torpadie was a very soothing preacher, but no one slept o'sermons during the reign of that pulpit cloth.

Mrs. Budlong was so elated over the success of it, however, that she announced her intention of going in for stained glass. She planned a series of the sweetest windows to replace those already in the church. But she never got nearer to that than painted china.

The painted china era was a dire era. The cups would break and the colors would run, and they never came out what she expected after they were fired. Of course she knew that the pigments must suffer alteration in the furnace, but there was always a surprise beyond surprise.

She soon became accustomed to getting green roses with crimson leaves, and deep blue apple blossoms against a pure white sky, but when she finished one complete set of table china in fifty pieces, each cup and saucer with a flower on it, the result looked so startlingly like something from a medical museum, that she never dared give the set away. She lent it to the cook to eat her meals on. The set went fast.

During this epoch Master Ulysses Budlong Jr. was studying at school a physiology ornamented with a few pictures in color representing the stomachs of alcohol specialists. They were intended, perhaps, to frighten little school children from frequenting saloons during recess, or to warn them not to put whisky on their porridge.

It was at this time that Mrs. Budlong spent two weeks' hard labor painting Easter lilies on an umbrella jug. When it came home from the furnace, her husband stared at it and mumbled:

"It's artistic, but what is it?"

Little Ulysses shrieked: "Oh, I know!" and darting away, returned with his physiology opened at one of those gastric sunsets, and—well, it was this that impelled Mrs. Budlong to a solemn pledge never to paint china again—a pledge she has nobly kept.

From smeared china she went to that art in which a woman buys something at a store, pulls out half of it, and calls the remnant drawn work. A season of this was succeeded by a mania for sofa cushions. It fairly snowed sofa cushions all over Carthage that Christmas; and Yale,

Harvard and Princeton pillows could be found in homes that had never known even a night school alumnus.

There ensued a sober period of burnt wood and a period of burnt leather, during which excited neighbors with a keen sense of smell called the fire department three times and the board of health once. And now Indian heads broke out all over town and the walls looked as if a shoemaker's apron had been chosen for the national pennant.

There were various other spasms of manufacture, each of them fashionable at its time and foolish at anytime. As Mr. Detwiller said:

"Somebody ought to write a history of Mrs. Budlong's Christmas presents. It would tell the complete story of all the darned fool fads that American women have been up to for twenty years."

But foolish soever, Mrs. Budlong was fair. A keen sense of sportsmanship led her to give full notice to such people as she planned to honor with her gifts. She knew how embarrassing it is to receive presents from one to whom no present has been sent, and she made it a point of honor somehow to forewarn her prospective beneficiaries betimes. Her favorite method was the classic device of pretending to let slip a secret. For instance:

"Yesterday morning, my dear, I had the strangest experience. It was just ten o'clock. I remember the hour so exactly because for the last few days I have made it a rule to begin work on your Christmas present just at ten— Oh, but I didn't mean to tell you. It was to be a surprise. No, don't ask me, I won't give you an inkling, but I really think it will please you. It's something you've been needing for such a long time."

And she left the victim to writhe from then on to Christmas, trying alternately to imagine what gift was impending and what would be an appropriate counter-gift.

III

MISTRESS OF THE REVELS

In more ways than one Mrs. Budlong kept Carthage on the writhe. Christmas was merely the climax of a ceaseless activity. All the year round she was at work like a yeast alert in a soggy dough.

She was forever getting up things. She was one of those terrible women who return calls on time or a little ahead. That made it necessary for you to return hers earlier. If you didn't, she called you up on the telephone and asked you why you hadn't. You had to promise to come over at once or she'd talk to you till your ear was welded to the telephone. Then if you broke your promise she called you up about that. She got in from fifty-two to a hundred and four calls a year, where one or two would have amply sufficed for all she had to say.

It was due to her that Carthage had such a lively social existence—for its size. Once, when she fell ill, the people felt suddenly as passengers feel when a street car is suddenly braked back on its haunches. All Carthage found itself wavering and poised on tiptoe and clinging to straps; and then it sogged back on its heels and waited till the car should resume progress. Mrs. Budlong was the town's motorman—or "motorneer," as they say in Carthage.

Before she was out of bed, she had invitations abroad for a convalescent tea, and everybody said, "Here we go again!"

If strangers visited Carthage, Mrs. Budlong counted them her clients the moment they arrived. Of course, the merely commercial visitors she left to the hackmen at the station, but friends or relatives of prominent people could not escape Mrs. Budlong's well-meant attentions. It was sometimes embarrassing when relatives appeared—for everybody has Concealed Relatives that he is perfectly willing to leave in concealment.

Mrs. Alex. (pronounced Ellick) Stubblebine never forgave Mrs. Budlong for dragging into the limelight some obscure cousins of her husband's who had drifted into Carthage to borrow money on their farm. Mrs. Stubblebine was always bragging about her people, her own people that is. Her husband's people, of course, were after all only Stubblebines, while her maiden name was Dilatush; and the Dilatushes, as everybody knew, were related by marriage to the Tatums.

But these were Stubblebines that came to town. Mrs. Stubblebine could hardly slam the door in their faces, but she would fain have locked the doors after them. She would not even invite them out on the front porch. She told them the back porch was cosier and less conspicuous. And then Mrs. Budlong had to call up on the telephone and sing out in her telephoniest tone:

"Oh, my dear, I've just this minute heard you have guests—some of your dear husband's relatives. Now they must come to me to dinner to-morrow. Oh, it isn't the slightest trouble, I assure you. I'm giving a little party anyway. I won't take no for an answer."

And she wouldn't. Mrs. Stubblebine fairly perspired excuses, but Mrs. Budlong finally grew so suspicious that she had to accept; or leave the impression that the relatives were burglars or counterfeiters in hiding. And they were not—they were pitifully honest.

The result was even worse than she feared. Mr. Stubblebine's cousin was so shy that he never said a word except when it was pulled out of him, and then he said, "Yes, ma'am"!

In Carthage when you are at a dinner party and you don't quite catch the last remark, you don't snap "What?" or "How?" or "Wha' jew say?" Whatever your home habits may be, at a dinner party or before comp'ny, you raise your eyebrows gracefully and murmur, "I beg your pardon."

But Mr. Stubblebine's rural cousin grunted "Huh?"—like an Indian chief trying to scare a white general. And he was perfectly frank about the intimate processes of mastication.

And when he dropped a batch of scalloped oysters into his watch pocket he solemnly fished them-out with a souvenir after-dinner coffee spoon having the Statue of Liberty for a handle and Brooklyn Bridge in the bowl.

And the wretch's wife was so nervous that she talked all the time about people the others had never seen or heard of. And she said she "never used tomattus." And she wasn't ashamed of what she was chewing either.

Mrs. Stubblebine would have felt much obliged to fate if she had been presented with an apoplectic stroke. But she had to sit the dinner out. From what she said to her poor husband afterward, however, one might have gathered that he picked out those relatives just to spite her, when as a matter of fact he had always loathed them and regretted them and the next day he borrowed enough money to lend them and send them back to the soil.

Mrs. Budlong had constituted herself Entertainment Committee for all sorts of visitors. If a young girl came home from boarding school with a classmate, the real hostess had hardly time to show her to the spare room, and say, "This is the bathroom, round here; watch out for the step. And if the water don't run just wait—" when the telephone would go Brrrr! And there would be Mrs. Budlong brandishing an invitation to a dinner party.

When the supply of guests ran low she would visit the sick. If a worn-out housewife slept late some morning to catch up, Mrs. Budlong would hear of it and rush over with a broth or something. It is said that old Miss

Malkin got out of bed with an unfinished attack of pneumonia, just to keep from eating any more of Mrs. Budlong's wine jellies.

In Carthage one pays for the telephone by the year. The company lost money on Mrs. Budlong's wire. As a telephoner she was simply interminable. She would spend a weekend at the instrument while the prisoner at the other extreme of the wire shifted from ear to ear, sagged along the wall, postponed household duties, made signals of distress to other members of the family, and generally cursed Mr. Alexander Graham Bell for his ingenuity.

Three wall telephones were changed to table phones on Mrs. Budlong's account, and Mrs. Talbot had hers put by the bed. She used to take naps while Mrs. Budlong talked and she trained herself to murmur, "Yes, dear," at intervals in her sleep.

By means like this Mrs. Budlong kept Carthage more or less under her thumb. Carthage squirmed but it could not crawl out from under.

This is the story of how the thumb was removed for good and all. It was Mrs. Budlong herself that removed it. Carthage could never have pried it up.

And strange to say the thumb came off because it grew popular.

Hitherto Mrs. Budlong had never been truly popular. People were merely afraid of her. She was a whipper-in, a social bush-beater, driving the populace from cover like partridges. She would not let the town rest. The merchants alone admired her, for she was the cause of much buying of new shoes, new hats, new clothes, fine groceries, olives, Malaga grapes, salted almonds, raisins, English walnuts and other things that one eats only at parties. She was the first woman in Carthage that ever gave a luncheon and called it breakfast, as years before she had been the first hostess to give a dinner at any time except in the middle of the day. Also, she was the first person there to say, "Come to me" when she meant "Come to our house." It had a Scriptural sound and was thought shocking until Carthage grew used to it.

It was due to her that several elderly men were forced into their first evening dress. They had thought to escape through life without that ordeal. Old Clute would have preferred to be fitted for a pine box, and would have felt about as comfortable in it. He tried to compromise with the tailor on a garment that could serve as a Prince Albert by day and a "swaller tail" by night, but Mr. Kweskin could not manage it even though his Christian name was Moses.

So Mr. Clute blamed Mrs. Budlong for yet another expense. Husbands all over town were blaming Mrs. Budlong for running their families into fool extravagances. Mothers were blaming her for dragging them round by the nose and leaving them no rest. But everybody in town resentfully obeyed Mrs. Budlong, though Mrs. Roscoe Detwiller wanted to organize a HomeKeepers Union, and strike. For the women never dared trust themselves about the house in a wrapper, since Mrs. Budlong might happen in as like as not—rather liker than not.

And then, just as the town was fermenting for revolt, Mrs. Budlong came into a lot of money.

IV

ONLY A MILLIONAIRE

That is, Mr. Budlong came into a lot of money. Which meant that Mr. Budlong would be permitted to take care of it while his wife got rid of it. One of those relatives, very common in fiction, and not altogether unknown in real life, finally let go of her money at the behest of her impatient undertaker. The Budlongs had the pleasure of seeing the glorious news of their good fortune in big headlines in the Carthage papers.

It was the only display Mr. Budlong ever received in that paper without paying for it—excepting the time when he ran for Mayor on the opposition ticket and was referred to in letters an inch high as "Candidate Nipped-in-the-Budlong."

But now the cornucopia of plenty had burst wide open on the front porch. It seemed as if they would have to wade through gold dollars to get to their front gate—when the money was collected. When the money was collected.

And now it was Mrs. Budlong's telephone that rang and rang. It was she that was called up and called up. It was she that sagged along the wall and shifted from foot to foot, from elbow to elbow and ear to ear.

After living in Carthage all her life she was suddenly, as it were, welcomed to the city as a distinguished visiting stranger. And now she had no need to invite people to return their calls. They came spontaneously. Sometimes there were a dozen calling at once. It was a reception every day. There were overflow meetings in the room which Mrs. Budlong called Mr. Budlong's "den." This was the place where she kept the furniture that she didn't dare keep in the parlor.

People who had never come to see her in spite of her prehensile telephone, dropped in to pay up some musty old call that had lain unreturned for years. People who had always come formally, even funereally, rushed in as informally and with as devouring an enthusiasm as old chums. People who used to run in informally now drove up in vehicles from MacMulkin's livery stable; or if they came in their own turn-outs they had the tops washed and the harness polished, and the gardener and furnaceman who drove, had his hat brushed, was not allowed to smoke, and was urged to sit up straight and for heaven's sake to keep his foot off the dashboard.

People who had been in the habit of devoting a day or two to cleaning up a year's social debts and went up and down the streets dropping doleful calls like wreaths on headstones, walked in unannounced of mornings. It was now Mrs. Budlong that had to keep dressed up all day. Everybody accepted the inevitable invitations to have a cup of tea, till the cook struck. Cook said she had conthracted to cuke for a small family, not to run a continurous bairbecue. Besides she had to answer the doorbell so much she couldn't get her hands into the dough, before they were out again. And dinner was never ready. The amount of tea consumed and bakery cake and the butter, began to alarm Mrs. Budlong. And Carthage people were so nervous at taking tea with a millionairess that they kept dropping cups or setting saucers down too hard.

Mrs. Budlong had never a moment the whole day long to leave the house, and she suddenly found herself without a call returned. She had so many invitations to dinners and luncheons, that her life became a hop, skip and jump.

During the first ecstasy of the good news, Mrs. Budlong had raved over the places she was going to travel,—Paris (now pronounced Paree), London, Vienna, St. Marks, the Lion of Lucerne—she talked like a handbook of Cook's Tours. To successive callers she told the story over and over till the rhapsody finally palled on her own tongue. She began to hate Paree, London, Vienna, St. Marks, and to loathe the Lion of Lucerne. All she wanted to do was to get out of town to some quiet retreat. Carthage was no longer quiet. It simmered to the boiling-over point.

Once it had been Mrs. Budlong's pride to be the social leader of Carthage. Now that her husband was worth (or to be worth) a hundred thousand dollars Carthage seemed a very petty parish to be the social leader of. She began to read New York society notes with expectancy, as one cons the Baedeker of a town one is approaching.

She lay awake nights wondering what she should wear at Mrs. Stuyvesant Square's next party and at Mrs. Astor House's sociable. She fretted the choice whether she should take a letter from her church to St. Bartholomew's or to Grace or St. John's the Divine's. And all the while she was pouring tea for the wives of harness makers and druggists, dentists and grocers.

The more reason for not appearing before them in the same clothes incessantly. But with a dinner or a reception or a tea or a ball every night, her two dressy-up dresses became so familiar that at one party when she was coming downstairs from laying off her cloak people spoke to her dress before they could see her face. And she could hardly afford to get new clothes, for after all she had not come into the money. She had just come at it, or toward it; or as her husband began to say, tip against it.

Mr. Budlong was kept on such tenterhooks by lawyers and papers to sign, titles to clear, executors and executrices to consult, and waivers, deeds, indentures and things that he had no time for his regular business.

As there is housemaid's knee, and painter's colic, so there is millionaire's melancholia. And the Budlongs were enduring the illness without entertaining the microbe.

It is almost as much trouble to inherit money nowadays as to earn it in the first place. Mr. Budlong was confronted with such a list of post-mortem debts that must be postpaid for his deceased Aunt Ida that he almost begrudged her her bit of very real estate in Woodlawn. And the Budlongs began to think that tombstones were in bad form if ostentatious. Heirs have notoriously simple tastes in monuments.

They had always accounted Aunt Ida a hard-fisted miser before, but now she began to look like a slippery-palmed spendthrift. They began almost to suspect the probity of the poor old maid. Worse yet, they feared that a later will might turn up bequeathing all her money to some abominable charity or other. She had been addicted to occasional subscriptions during her lifetime.

The Budlongs themselves were beginning, even at this distance from their money-to-be, to suffer its infection, its inevitable reaction on the character. Those who live beyond their means joyously when their means are small, become small themselves, when their means get beyond living beyond. The Budlongs began to figure percentages on sums left in the bank or put out on mortgages. They began to think money; and money is money, large or small. Mrs. Budlong began to feel that she had been unjust to Aunt Ida. What she had called miserliness was really prudence and thrift and other pleasant-sounding virtues. What she had called liberality was wanton waste.

Finally her social debts reached such a mass that she decided to give a large dinner to wipe off a great number at once. But now when she calculated that the olives, the turkey, the Malaga grapes, the English walnuts, the salted almonds and a man from the hotel to wait on table, would total up twenty-five dollars or so, she found herself figuring how much twenty-five dollars would amount to in twenty-five years at compound interest.

She grew frantic to be quit of Carthage—to rub it off her visiting list. Unconsciously her motto became Cato's ruthless *Carthago delenda est*.

But she could neither delete Carthage from her map, nor free her feet from its dust. Her husband's business required him yet awhile. Even to close it up took time. And he would not, and could not, borrow money on Aunt Ida's estate till he was sure that it was his.

But all the while the festival reveled on. People in Carthage to whom New York was an inaccessible Carcassone, were now planning to visit Mrs. Budlong there at the palatial home she had described. Some of them frankly told her they were coming to see her. Wealth took on a new discomfort.

Sally Swezey afflicted the telephone with gossip: "As Mrs. Talbot was saying only yes'day, my dear, so many folks have threatened to visit you in your home on Fifth Avenue that you'll have to hang hammocks in your front yard."

And now they had spoiled even her future for her. What pride could she take in having a gorgeous home on Fifth Avenue with all these Carthage people rocking on the front porch. Probably some warm evening when Mrs. Hotel Vanderbilt was driving by in her new barouche, it would be just like Roscoe Detwiller to turn in at the gate, flounce down on the top step and sit there with his vest unbuttoned, and his seersucker coat under his arm, while he mopped the inside of his hat with his handkerchief.

But that was the discomfort of the morrow. To-day had its own spawn. One morning she was called to the telephone by the merciless Sallie

Swezey with a new infliction. There was something almost ghoulish in Mrs. Swezey's cackling glee as she sang out across the wire:

"We're all so glad, my dear, that the next meeting of the Progressive Euchre is to be at your house."

Mrs. Budlong's chin dropped. She had quite forgotten this. Sallie chortled on:

"And say, do you know what?"

"What?"

"Everybody says you're going to give solid gold prizes and that even your booby prize will be handsomer than the first prize was at Mrs. Detwiller's."

"Ha, ha!" laughed Mrs. Budlong in a tone that sounded just like the spelling.

Mrs. Budlong's wealth seemed to be accepted as a sort of municipal legacy. All Carthage assumed to own it in community, and to enjoy it with her. Her walls rang with the hilarity of her neighbors. But her laughter took on more and more the sound of icicles snapping from the eaves of a shed.

She became the logical candidate for all the chief offices in clubs and societies and circles. She suddenly found herself seven or eight presidents and at least eleven chairwomen. The richest woman in town heretofore was Mrs. Foster Herpers, wife of the pole and shaft manufacturer. He owned about half of the real estate in town, but his wife had to distill expenses out of him in pennies. With a profound sigh of relief she resigned all her honors in Mrs. Budlong's favor.

Being president chiefly meant lending one's house for meetings as well as one's china and tea and sandwiches, and being five dollars ahead of anybody else in every subscription. Mrs. Budlong was panic-stricken with her own success, for there is nothing harder to handle than a dam-break of prosperity.

Worse yet, Mr. Budlong was ceasing to be the meek thing of yore. Every day was the first of the month with him.

It was well on in November when he flung himself into a Morris chair one evening and groaned aloud:

"I don't believe Aunt Ida ever left any money. If she did I don't believe we'll ever get any of it. And if we do, I know we'll not have a sniff at it before January. One of the lawyers has been called abroad on another case. We've got to stay in Carthage, at least over Christmas."

"Christmas!" The word crackled and sputtered in Mrs. Budlong's brain like a fuse in the dark. The past month had been so packed with other excitements that she had forgotten the very word. Now it blew up and came down as if one of her own unstable Christmas trees had toppled over on her with all its ropes of tinsel, its lambent tapers, and its eggshell splendors.

V

THE BITER BIT

First, Mrs. Budlong felt amazement that she could have so ignored the very focus of her former ambition. Then she felt shame at her unpreparedness. She caught the evening paper out of her husband's lap to find the date. November ninth and not a Christmas thing begun. Yet a few days and the news-stands would have apprised her that Christmas was coming, for by the middle of November all the magazines put on their holly and their chromos of the three Magi and their Santa Clauses, as women put on summer straw hats at Easter.

Mrs. Budlong's hands sought and wrung each other as if in mutual reproach. They had been pouring tea and passing wafers when they should have been Dorcassing at their Christmas tasks. It had been left for her husband of all people to warn her that her own special Bacchanal was imminent.

If he had been a day later, the neighbors would have anticipated him as well as the magazines. The Christmas idea seemed to strike the whole town at once. Mrs. Budlong became the victim of her own classic device of pretending to let slip a secret. The townswomen shamelessly turned her own formula against her.

Mrs. Detwiller met her at church and said:

"Yesterday morning at eleven I had the most curious presentiment, my dear. I remember the hour so exactly because I've been making it a rule to begin work on your Christmas present every morning at— Oh, but I didn't inTend to let you know. No, dearie, I won't tell you what it is. But I can't help believing it's Just what you'll need in New York."

Myra Eppley, with whom Mrs. Budlong had never exchanged Christmas presents, at all, but with whom an intimacy had sprung up since Mrs. Budlong came into the reputation of her money—Myra Eppley had the effrontery to call up on the telephone and say:

"Would you mind telling me, my dear, the shade of wall paper you're going to have in your New York parlor, because I'm making you the daintiest little—well, no matter, but will you tell me?"

Poor Mrs. Budlong almost swooned from the telephone. She did not know what the color of her wall paper would be in New York. She did not know that she would ever have wall paper in New York. She only knew that Myra Eppley, too, was calling her "my dear." Myra Eppley also was going to give her a Christmas present. And would have to be given one.

Mrs. Budlong had received fair warning, but she felt about as grateful as a wayfarer feels to the rattlesnake that whizzes "Make r-r-r-ready for the corrroner-r-r."

Next, young Mrs. Chur (Editha Cinnamon as was, for she had finally landed Mr. Chur in spite of the accident—or because of it) called up to say:

"Oh, my dear, my husband wants to know what brand of cigars your husband smokes; and would you tell me, dearie—it's rather personal, but—what size bath-slippers you wear?"

When Sally Swezey came to the Progressive Euchre skirmish at Mrs. Budlong's she noted with joy that her hint had borne fruit. The prizes were indeed of solid gold. Mr. Budlong did not learn it till the first of the following month when the bill came in from Jim Henderson's jewelry store.

As if she had not done enough in forcing solid gold prizes on Mr. Budlong, Sally had to say:

"I'm just dying to see your back parlor, my dear, this next Christmas afternoon. It has always been a sight for sore eyes; but this Christmas it will be a perfect wonder, for I do declare everybody in town is going to send you something nice."

This conviction was already chilling Mrs. Budlong's marrow. Of old she would have rejoiced at the golden triumph, but now she could only realize that if everybody in Carthage sent her something nice, it was because everybody in Carthage expected something nicer. And her Christmas crops were hopelessly backward. At a time when she should be half done, she could not even begin. She had not tatted or smeared or hammered a thing.

VI

DESPAIR AND AN IDEA

Days and days went by in a stupor of dull hopelessness. Thanksgiving came and the Budlong turkey might as well have been a crow. In desperation she decided to make a tentative exploration of the shops now burgeoning with Christmas splendor; every window a spasm of gewgaws. Since she had no time to make, she must buy.

The length of her list sent her to the cheaper counters, but she was not permitted to browse among them. At Strouther and Streckfuss's, Mr. Strouther came up and said with reeking unctuousness:

"Vat is Mees Bootlonk doink down here amonkst all this tresh? Come see our importet novelties."

And he led her to a region where the minimum price was MBBA-BDJA, which meant that it cost 12.25 and could be safely marked down to 23.75.

She eluded him and got back to the 25-cent realm only to be apprehended by Mr. Streckfuss, who beamed:

"Ah, nothink is here for a lady like you are. Only fine kvality suits such a taste you got."

By almost superfeminine strength she evaded purchasing anything. She went to other shops only to be haled to the expensive counters. Storekeepers simply would not discuss cheap things with the millionairess-elect.

She crept home and threw herself on her husband's mercy. He had none and she lighted hard. It was the first of December, and in addition to his monthly rage, Mr. Budlong was working himself up to his regular pre-

Christmas frenzy, when he always felt poor and talked poorer to keep the family in check.

His face was a study when he had heard his wife's state of mind. Forthwith he delivered the annual address on Christmas folly that one hears from fathers of families all round the world at this time:

"Christmas has quit being a sign of people's affections," Mr. Budlong thundered. "It has become a public menace. It's worse than Wall Street. Wall Street is supposed have started as the thermometer of the country's business and now it's gone and got so goldum big that the thermometer is makin' the weather. When Wall Street feels muggy it's got to rain and the sun don't dare shine without takin' a peek at the thermometer first off.

"Christmas ain't any longer an opportunity to show good will to your neighbors. It's a time when you got to show off before your neighbors. You women make yourselves and us men sick the way you carry on all through December. And the children!—they're worse'n the grown-ups.

"Old-fashioned Christmas was like old-fashioned circuses—mostly meant for the young ones. Nowadays circuses have growed so big and so improper that nobody would dast take a child to one, or if you do, they get crazy notions.

"When I was a boy, if I got a drum and a tin horn I was so happy I couldn't keep quiet. But last Christmas little Ulie Junior cried all day because he got a 'leven dollar automobile when he wanted a areaplane big enough to carry the cat over the barn.

"This Christmas trust business ought to be investigated by the gov'ment and dissolved. Talk about your tariff schedules! What we need is somebody to pare down this Christmas gouge. It's the one kind of tax you can't swear off.

"And as for you—why, you're goin' daffy. Other years I didn't mind so much. You spent a lot of time and some money on your annual splurge, but I will say, you took in better'n you gave. But now you're on the other side the fence. These Carthage women have got you on the run. You'll have to give 'em twice as good as they send or you're gone. You're gone anyway. If you gave each one of 'em a gold platter full of diamonds they'd say you'd inherited Aunt Ida's stinginess as well as her money."

Mrs. Budlong went on twisting her fingers: "Oh, of course you're right, Ule. But what's the use of being right when it's so hateful? All I can think of is that Everybody in town is going to give me a present! Everybody!"

"Can't you take your last year's presents and pass 'em along to other folks?"

"Everybody would recognize them, and I'd be the talk of the town."

"You're that anyway, so what difference does it make?"

"I'd rather die."

"You'd save a lot of money and trouble if you did."

"Just look at the list of presents I must give."

She handed him a bundle of papers. He pushed up his spectacles and put on his reading glasses, and instantly snorted:

"Say! What is this? the town directory?"

He had not read far down the list when he missed one important name. "You've overlooked Mrs. Alsop."

"Oh, her! I've quarreled with her. We don't speak, thank heaven."

"It would be money in your pocket, if you didn't speak to anybody. Gosh!" he slapped his knee. "I have an idea. Stop speaking to everybody."

"Don't be silly."

"I mean it."

VII

FOILED

Ulysses S. G. Budlong was a man fertile in ideas and unflinching in their execution. Otherwise he would never have attained his present unquestioned supremacy, as the leading hay and feed merchant in Carthage.

"It's as easy as falling off a log," he urged. "You women are always spatting about something. Now's your chance to capitalize your spats."

"Men are such im-boo-hoo-ciles!" was Mrs. Budlong's comment, as she began to weep. Her husband patted her with a timid awkwardness as if she were the nose of a strange horse. "There! there! we'll fix this up fine. What did you quarrel with Mrs. Alsop about?"

"She told Sally Swezey and Sally Swezey told me—that I used my Carthage presents to send to relatives in other towns."

"She flattered you at that," said Mr. Budlong unconsolingly. "But don't you dream of forgiving her till after Christmas."

Mrs. Budlong was having such a good cry, and enjoying the optical hath so heartily, that her grief became very precious to her. It suggested what a beautiful thing grief is to those who make a fine art of it.

She smiled wet-liddedly. "There is nothing in your idea, Ulie, but it has suggested a good one to me. I'll announce that I can't celebrate Christmas because of our great grief for Aunt Ida."

"Great grief!" Mr. Budlong echoed. "Why, you couldn't have celebrated Aunt Ida's finish more joyous without you'd serenaded her in Woodlawn with a brass band."

"Ulysses Budlong! you ought to be ashamed of yourself for saying such a thing!" But she suddenly heard, in fancy, the laugh that would go up if she sprung such an excuse. She gave in:

"We'll have to quarrel with somebody then. But what excuse is there?"

"Women don't need any real excuse. You simply telephone Sally Swezey that a certain person told you—and you won't name any names—that she had been making fun of you and you'd be much obliged if she never spoke to you again for you'd certainly never speak to her again."

"But how do I know Sally Swezey has been making fun of me?"

"Oh, there ain't any doubt but what everybody in town is doing that."

"Ulysses Budlong! how can you talk so!"

"If people without money couldn't make fun of people with—what consolation would they have? Anyway, it's not me but the other folks you're supposed to quarrel with. You spend an hour at that telephone and you can get the whole town by the ears."

"But I can't use the same excuse for everybody."

"You'll think up plenty once you put your mind to it." And with that another excuse came in pat. Came in howling and flagrant.

Ulysses Junior burst into the room, as if he had forgotten the presence of the door. He was yelping like a coyote and from his tiny nose an astonishing amount of blood was spouting.

"What on earth is the matter!" the startled mother gasped. "Come here to me, you poor child—-and be careful not to bleed on the new rug."

Ulysses' articulation was impeded with sobs and the oscillations of three semi-detached teeth, that waved in the breeze as he screamed: "Little Clarence Detwiller LICKED me! so he did! and I on'y p-pushed him off his sled into a puddle of ice wa-wa-water and he attackted me and kicked my f-f-Face-ace off."

Mr. and Mrs. Budlong were so elated with the same idea that they forgot to console their heart-broken offspring with more than Mr. Budlong's curt, "First teeth anyway; saves you a trip to the dentist." He nodded to his wife.

"Just the excuse we were looking for."

"Sent direct from heaven," nodded Mrs. Budlong. "You call up Roscoe Detwiller this minute and tell him his son has criminal tendencies and ought to be in jail and will undoubtedly die on the gallows. Then he won't speak to you to-morrow."

"You bet he won't. He'll just quietly do to me what his boy did to Ulie. No, my dear, you tell all that to Mrs. Detwiller yourself."

Mrs. Budlong tossed her head with fine contempt. "What cowards men are! always shielding themselves behind women's skirts. Well, if you're afraid, I'm not. I'll give her the biggest talking to she ever had in her born days."

She rose with fortitude and started to the telephone, sneered at it and glared at it. Her husband stood by her to support her in the hour of need. He watched her ask for the number, and snap ferociously at the central. Then she fell panicky again and held the transmitter to him appealingly. He waved her away scornfully.

She set her teeth hard and there was grimness in her eye and tone as she said: "Is this you, Mrs. Detwiller! —— Oh, yes, thank you, I'm very well. I wanted to tell you-m —— oh, yes, he's well, too. But what I started to say was —— Yes, so Ulie says! ——— Yes, right in the face ——— Oh, of course, ——— Naturally ——— Boys will be ——— ——— Oh, I'm sorry you punished him. He's such a sweet child ——— ——— Oh, don't think of it. I'm sure it was all Ulie's fault. It will teach him better next time. He's so rough! ——— ——— Oh, really, how awfully sweet of you. Good night, dear."

She stuck the receiver on the hook and looked for a hook to hang herself on. Her eyes were shifty with shame as she mumbled:

"I couldn't get a word in edgeways. She apologized."

"She apologized!" Mr. Budlong roared. "Why, you ate out of her hand. And you were going to show me what a coward I— Butter wouldn't have melted—say, why didn't you kiss her?"

Mrs. Budlong was suffering a greater dismay than remorse. "What d'you suppose that cat of a Clara Detwiller's going to do?" she moaned. "She's going to make her boy send Ulie a nice Christmas present! And now we'll have to buy one for Ulie to give to him!"

"Well, of all the—oh, you're a great manager, you are! You call up a woman to get rid of giving one Christmas present, and now you've got to give two. Here! where you going?"

"I'm going to that phone and tell Mrs. Detwiller what I think of her."

"You keep away from that phone. Before you could ring off again her husband would have a Christmas present wished onto ME!"

VIII

FOILED AGAIN

The next morning Mrs. Budlong arose from dreams of finding bargains after all. She felt a spirit in her feet that led her, who knows how, to the Christmas-window street. But the crowds and the prices and the servility of the salesfolk drove her out again.

On her laggard way home she saw Sally Swezey, lean and lanky and somehow reminding her of a flamingo. Sally espied her from afar and stepped a little higher. Mrs. Budlong remembered her husband's suggestion. She made a quick resolution to do or die. Her cheek was cold and white and her heart beat loud and fast, but she tried to set her double chin into a square jaw, and she passed Sally Swezey as if Sally Swezey were a lamp-post by the curb—a common lamp-post by the curb, and nothing more.

She heard Sally's gush of greeting stop short as if someone had turned a faucet in her throat; she heard a gulp; then she heard a strangled silence. Then she heard Sally call her name tentatively, tenderly, reproachfully. Then she heard no more. And she knew no more till her feet somehow carried her home. But she had hardly time to flop into a rocker and utter a prayer of gratitude and pride for having been vouchsafed the courage to snub a Carthaginian before Br-r-rr!—the relentless telephone was on her trail. She knew just who it was and she braced herself to meet one of Sally's sharp-tongued assaults. But Sally said—in part:

"Oh, you poor darling dear, is that you? And how are you now? I was so alarmed for you. You looked so ill and worn and—aren't the Christmas crowds awful this year? And nothing fit to buy and such prices! And— you must be just worn out. You really must spare yourself, for do you know what you Did, dearest. You went right By me without Seeing me, or Answering me! Yes, you did! I was so startled that I didn't have brains enough to run after you and assist you home. I'm so glad you got there alive and I Do hope you're feeling better and I'm so aShamed of myself for letting you go all that way aLone in that pitiful conDition. Can you ever forGive me?"

When Mr. Budlong came home for luncheon, Mrs. Budlong told him the whole story. He glared at her with an I-give-you-up expression and growled:

"And when she said all that, what did you say?"

"I don't know." Mrs. Budlong faltered. "All I know is that she's coming over this afternoon with a lot of that wine jelly I gave her the receipt for."

"And what do you intend to do this time?" Mr. Budlong demanded. The skeptic in his tone stung her to revolt. She could usually be strong in the presence of her husband. She looked at least like Mrs. Boadicea as she said:

"I intend to tell Sally Swezey what you told me to. And I will accept no apologies, none whatever."

When Mr. Budlong came home to dinner she avoided his gaze. She confessed that she had changed her program. She hadn't the heart to insult poor Sally, and she had admitted that she was a hit dizzy and qualmish and she had—well, she—she—

Mr. Budlong finished for her fiercely:

"I know! You ate a lot of her wine jelly, and you told her she was a love and you kissed her good-by, and would she excuse you from coming to the door because you were still a little wobbly."

Mrs. Budlong looked at him in surprise: "She told you!"

"Nah! I haven't seen her."

"Then how on earth did you ever guess?" she babbled.

"It was my womanly intuition!" he snarled, and that evening he went down town and sat in the hotel lobby for a couple of hours. He usually did this anyway—in summer he sat on the sidewalk—but this evening, he did it with a certain implication of escape. He expressed renunciation in the mere shutting of the door.

On the way home Mr. Budlong was busy with schemes. His mind turned again to his son.

In a smallish town, a growing boy is an unfailing source of casus belli.

As an inciter of feuds there was something almost Balkan or Moroccan about Ulysses Budlong Junior. Nearly every day he had come charging into the house with bad news in some form or other. Some rock or snowball he had cast with the most innocent of intentions had gone through a window or a milk wagon or somebody's silk hat. Or he had pulled a small girl's hair, or taken the skates away from a helpless urchin. He had bad luck too in picking victims with belligerent big brothers.

Mr. Budlong recognized these desperado traits and he fully expected Ulysses Junior to make him the father of a convict. Suddenly now despair became hope. Let Mrs. Budlong capitalize her spats; he would promote Ulie's. The affair Detwiller had turned out badly, but Mr. Budlong would not yield to one defeat. He watched eagerly for the next misdemeanor of his young hopeless. He relied on him to embroil, as it were, all Europe in an international conflict.

But the dove of peace seemed to have alighted on Ulysses' shoulder. He even began to go to Sunday School—the Methodist this year because they had given the largest cornucopias in town the Christmas before. And he talked nothing but Golden Texts till Mr. Budlong began to fear that he would one day be the father of a parson.

Meanwhile, Mrs. Budlong grew bellicose again. She snubbed people right and left, but they generously imputed it to absent-mindedness. She failed to go to the dinner party the Teeples gave in her honor, and she sent no excuse. This was the unpardonable sin in Carthage and the Budlong chairs sat vacant through the dinner.

But Mrs. Teeple graciously assumed that she was ill and sent over the cut flowers off the table. And she hoped the poor dear would feel better soon.

A few days later Mrs. Budlong's pet Maltese kitten was done to nine deaths at once by the Disney's fox terrier. Mrs. Budlong mourned the kitten, but there was consolation in the thought that she could now cut the Disneys off her list.

Before she could get the kitten decently interred in the back yard, Mrs. Disney was at the front door. She flung her arms round Mrs. Budlong and wept, declaring that she had resolved to give the murderous terrier away to a farmer, and had already sent to Chicago for a pedigreed Angora to replace the Maltese. It would arrive the day before Christmas.

IX

WORSE, AND MORE OF IT

As if that were not enough for one day, in the afternoon Johnetta Ackerley called. She saw Mrs. Budlong at an upper window and waved to her as she came along the walk. When the cook arrived upstairs like a grand piano moving in, Mrs. Budlong said in an icy tone:

"Not at home."

"But I told her you was. And she seen you at the windy."

"Not!—at!—home!"

"But I'm after telling her—"

Mrs. Budlong could be as stern as steel with her husband or her servants. She cowed Brigida into lumbering downstairs with the message. Mrs. Budlong went to the window to triumph over her victim's retreat in a panic of confusion.

Instead, she heard a light patter of footsteps and Johnetta Ackerley hurried into the room.

"Oh, my dear, are you ill? Pardon my coming right up, but the cook takes so long and I was so worried for fear you were—but you aren't, are you?"

Mrs. Budlong was at bay. She glared at the intruder and threw up her chin. Johnetta stared at her aghast.

"Why, my dear! You aren't mad at me, are you?"

Mrs. Budlong smiled bitterly, and said nothing. Johnetta shrilled:

"Why, what have I done?"

As a matter of fact, what had she done? All that Mrs. Budlong could think of was her husband's unused suggestion for a war with Sally Swezey. She spoke through locked teeth:

"It's not what you've done but what you've said."

"Why, what have I said?"

"You know well enough what you've been saying behind my back, and you needn't think that people don't come and tell me. I name no names, but I know! Oh, I know!"

Now, of course, everybody says things behind everybody else's back that nobody would care to have repeated to anybody. Through Johnetta Ackerley's memory dashed a hundred caustic comments she had made on Mrs. Budlong. She blushed and sighed, turned away and closed the door after her, like the last line of an elegy.

A surge of triumph swept over Mrs. Budlong. Success at last.

Then the door opened and Johnetta reappeared on the sill with a look of angelic contrition.

"I hardly know what to say," she said. "Of course, I must admit I did rather forget myself. It was at the last meeting of the Progressive Euchre Club and everybody was criticizing you for having solid gold prizes when they were at your house. They said it was vulgar ostentation. I didn't say anything for the longest time, but finally when they all said your money had gone to your head, hadn't it, I admit I did mumble, 'It seems so.' But it is only what everybody else says all the time, and I assure you I didn't really mean it. Of course nobody can behave just the same after they are a millionaire as they did before. But I am awfully fond of you and—and—"

"It was most disloyal," said Mrs. Budlong. "And to think that after tearing me to pieces behind my back, you could come and call on me."

It was a fine speech, but after she heard herself say it, Mrs. Budlong had a sinking feeling that if she herself had never called on anybody she had not criticized she would have stayed at home all her life. But Johnetta Ackerley took another line. She threw herself on Mrs. Budlong's mercy, and if Mrs. Budlong boasted of anything more than another it was her mercy.

"I have just been at the church," said Johnetta, "helping to decorate it for Christmas week, and I was hanging up a big motto 'Peace on Earth, Good Will to Men' and I think it ought to apply to women, too. I grovel in apology and I pray you to forgive me. You can't refuse your forgiveness when I implore it, can you?"

Mrs. Budlong wanted to but could not and the two women fell about each other's throats and exchanged moan for moan. As they were comfortably dabbing each other's tears from their cheeks and sniffing their own and laughing cosily after the rain, Johnetta giggled and sobbed at once.

"The idea of your thinking I didn't just love you—and me working my fingers to the bone making a Christmas present for you!"

X

A WELL-LAID PLAN

In the Civil War there were over two thousand battles and the details could not be reported in a lifetime. But their result can be stated in a phrase. The same brevity must apply to the campaigns, the stratagems, ballistics and tactics of Mrs. Budlong: numberless efforts at secession ended as a lost cause.

There was one more desperate struggle. While only a few days stood between her and her famous Christmas afternoons, she and her dour husband were having a bitter council of war. She had another attack of inspiration.

"I have it! the very thing! Why haven't we thought of it before? Quarantine!"

"Quarantine?" echoed Mr. Budlong as if the word were gibberish.

"Yes. If we had something contagious in the house and a quarantine on, people couldn't come here with their odious gifts and they would be so afraid to get ours that they'd be much obliged to us for not sending them any."

For the first time in years Mr. Budlong paid Mrs. Budlong a sincere homage:

"You're a genius. It takes a woman to squirm out of a difficulty after all."

He was so excited he actually kissed her—and he hadn't finished his evening paper at that!

This overjoyed her so far that she fairly glowed.

"Oh, I'm so glad you approve, Ulie dear. And you'll help me, won't you?"

"You bet I will, ducky dove."

"That's glorious. Now which will you pretend to have, yellow fever or smallpox or—"

"Which will *I* pretend to have? Do you mean to say that you expect ME to go bed with a fatal disease?"

"It doesn't have to be fatal, my love. Just so long as it's contagious, you know."

"Well, of all th—what's to happen to my business?"

"Why, you can call it a vacation. And you can pretend to get well after Christmas; or you can have the doctor say it wasn't yellow fever after all."

"But I stay in bed for several days, eh?"

"Oh, you can move round all you want, just so 's't you don't go outdoors, and keep away from the windows."

Mr. Budlong's admiration was reverting to its normal state. He growled:

"You women would be an awful joke, if you were only a little funnier. If you're so keen on this quarantine business you quarantine yourself. You can have yellow fever, or scarlet, or green or any color you like—robin's egg blue fever for all I care."

"But, my darling, I can't be having those things! You know I don't believe in them this year, since I became a—oh, it wouldn't do at all for Me. But You could have it because You believe in diseases."

"You bet I do, and I believe you've got softening of the brain." He paced the floor in an effort to keep up with his temper. Eventually he stopped short.

He remembered that his son had failed to help the family out in its distress. He said:

"Let Ulie have something."

XI

GANG AGLEY AGAIN

Mrs. Budlong felt a certain superstitious uneasiness, but was finally won over, and Ulie was unanimously elected the scapegoat—or in more modern form, the goat.

Ulie was in bed at the time sleeping like an innocent cherub and smiling in his sleep. He was dreaming of a great invention: he would set a figure-4 trap near his fireplace and snare Santa Claus by the foot. Then from a safe ambush under the bed, he would assail the old gentleman with his nigger-shooter till he laid him low, whereupon he could rifle the entire pack at his leisure, and select what he wanted. Ulie had not been attending Sabbath School in vain. The lesson of the week concerned David and Goliath.

From such dreams as these Ulie woke the next morning to be told that he need not leave his bed. He had scarlet fever and must keep close under his cover.

"Scarlet nothin'!" was Ulie's reply. "I gotter go to a meetin' of the Youth's Helpin' Hand Socirety this afternoon and I'll be darned if I stay in any dog-on bed."

Mr. Budlong finally persuaded him—Ulie wasn't dressed yet and it hurts worse on the bare hide. Then Mr. Budlong hurried down town to bribe a doctor and borrow a red placard of the board of health. He was just rounding the corner on the way home when he caught sight of Ulie descending from the window by means of a knotted sheet. Ulie had only a nightgown on, and owing to the heavy wind it wasn't much on.

He dropped to the ground before Mr. Budlong could reach him, then darted away across lots barefooted through the snow towards the

Detwillers'. Mr. Budlong treed him just before he reached the neighbors. But the boy would not come down till his father promised immunity both from punishment and from scarlet fever.

The Detwillers were arriving on the run, so the father promised, hid the scarlet fever propaganda in his inside pocket, wrapped Ulie in his own overcoat and carried him home. There was so much dread of pneumonia that the guilty parents could not include Ulie in any more schemes. And they could think of no schemes. The day before the Day Before Christmas found them in a panic. The Day Before found them grimly resolved to stand siege.

On the blessed Eve they sat before their cheerless fire-front and stared at the packages that had been pouring in all day long. The old postman had staggered under the final load and hinted so broadly for a Christmas present that he got one—the first breach in their solemn resolve.

They had excepted Ulie, of course, from the embargo. But they had been in such a flurry that they had postponed him till they forgot him entirely. The doorbell was rung so incessantly throughout the evening that the cook sat on the hall stairs to be handy. She piled the packages up on the piano till they spilled off. The piano lamp was gradually sinking beneath the encroaching tide. Presents were brought in wagons, carriages, buggies, carts, by coachmen, gardeners, cooks, maids, messenger boys, and children of all ages and dimensions.

On any other occasion Mrs. Budlong would have been running here and there, peeking into parcels and restraining her curiosity till the next day out of sheer joy in curiosity. Now she opened never a bundle. She could only think of the morrow when all of these donors found that reciprocity had gone down to defeat. The Budlongs avoided each other's eyes. They were thinking the same thing. The strain endured till it tested their metal to the breaking point. When three enormous packages were brought to the door by the Detwillers' hired man, Mrs. Budlong broke out hysterically:

"I just can't stand it."

"Hell!" roared Mr. Budlong. "Get on your hat and coat. We'll go down and buy everything that's left in town."

XII

AN AMAZING CHRISTMAS

Holiday bargains in Carthage were not brilliant. After being pawed over for several weeks, they were depressing indeed. When the Budlongs strode into Strouther and Streckfuss's, it was nearly ten o'clock at night. The sales-wretches, mostly pathetic spinsters of both sexes, were gaunt and jaded. They yawned incessantly and held on to the counters.

Even Messrs. Strouther and Streckfuss had the nap worn off their plushy sleekness. They were surveying the wreckage, and dolefully realizing that some of the Christmas bills would not be paid by the Fourth of July.

When the Budlongs made their irruption, they were not received cordially. Word had gone abroad that the Budlongs were buying all their Christmas presents out of town. They must be, for they bought none in. This treachery to home industry was bitterly resented. Then Budlong galvanized everybody with a cry like a flash of lightning:

"I want to buy nearly everything in the shop. Get busy."

It was too late to select. Mr. and Mrs. Budlong with their lengthy list in hand sprinted up one aisle and down another, pointing, prodding, rarely pausing to say "How much?" but monotonously chanting: "Gimme this! Gimme that! Gimme two of these! Gimme six of them! Gimme that! Gimme this! Gimme them!"

They bought glaring garden jars and ghastly vases, scarf pins that would disturb the peace, silly bisque figurines for mantels and what-nots, combs and brushes that would raise the hair on end instead of allaying it, oxidized silverized lead pencils, button hooks, tooth brushes, nail files, cuticle knives, pin cushions, ink stands, paper weights, picture frames, bits of lace and intimate white things with ribbons in them—Mr. Budlong turned away while she priced these.

Strouther and Streckfuss were in a panic of joy at the situation. They managed in the excitement to work off a number of old horrors that had been refused for years and years—ancient, dust-stained landmarks on the shelves. Mr. Strouther showed the things, Mr. Streckfuss wrote the list of purchases,—he made many mistakes in prices, but strangely never to his own damage; and the entire staff of assistants followed, taking down, and wrapping up, and rushing parcels to the door, where they were bundled onto a wagon.

Mr. Budlong should have been a medieval general. He pillaged that store with the thoroughness of the Crusaders looting Constantinople.

The town clock was striking midnight as the Budlongs dragged themselves home. There was much yet to be done. Parcels must be opened, price tags removed, gifts done up in pink tissue paper and gold twine, cards must be inscribed and inserted and the parcels rewrapped and addressed. The Strouther and Streckfuss driver had been hired at an exorbitant cost to sit up and deliver the gifts. The horses had not been consulted. They leaned on each other and slept, dreaming of oats.

The Budlong parlor was soon a hideous scene. The husband would open a bundle and sing out, "Who's this big immense pink and purple cuspidor for?"

"That's a jardineer," Mrs. Budlong would gasp. "It's a return for that horrible cat those hateful Disneys are going to inflict on me. Here's the card."

She handed him a holly-wreathed pasteboard on which she had written, "For Mr. and Mrs. Disney with most affectionate Yuletide greetings."

She indited cards as fast as she could think up phrases. She sought for variety, but the effort was maddening. She wrote, "Very merry Christmas," "The merriest of Xmases," "A merry merry Yuletide," "A Happy Christmas and a Merry New Year," "Christmas Greetings," "Xmas Greetings," "Yuletide Greetings," "Wishing you a—" "With loving wishes for—" "Affectionate," and so on and so on and on and on. She scribbled and scrawled till slumber drugged her and her pen went crazy. When she fell asleep she was writing "A Yuly Newmas and a Happy X-Year to Swally Sezey."

The delivery man pounded on the door and wild-eyed Budlong let him in from the night. The man whispered that he'd have to start at once if he was to make the rounds before his horses laid down on him.

Mr. Budlong called his wife, but she did not answer. He shook her and she threatened to roll off the chair on to a divan. Mr. Budlong straightened her out and gazed at her in hopeless pity. He stared at the chaos of bundles.

He seized the pack of cards from his wife's chubby fingers and ran here and there jabbing pasteboards into bundles, regardless.

That is how Myra Eppley acquired an ash tray lined with cigar bands, and why old Mr. Clute was amazed to receive a card offering him Mrs. Budlong's "loving and affectionate greetings." He was more amazed when he opened the bundle. It had ribbons in it.

There were other amazements in town the next morning. In fact, it was the amazingest Christmas Carthage had ever had.

As fast as Mr. Budlong stuffed cards into bundles, he loaded bundles into the driver's arms as if they were sticks of wood. The driver stacked them up in his wagon. He made seven trips in all and some of the cards fell out and were stuck in still wronger bundles than before. But both the driver and Mr. Budlong were too sleepy to care. The driver finally mounted his seat and called out from the dark:

"Say, Mr. Budlong, where do I leave these packages—on the porch, or do I ring the bell?"

"Chuck 'em through the windows! The more glass you break the better I'll like it."

"All right, sir. Get ap! Good night, sir, and wishing you a Merry Christmas!"

"Merry ———" said Mr. Budlong, reaching for a rock. But even the stones were frozen to the ground and the driver escaped. As Mr. Budlong closed his front door, a thread of crimson spun out along the East as if somebody were going to wrap the whole world up in a red string. He did not want it. He yawned at it.

An hour or so later, Ulie awoke and sat up with a start. To his intense confusion, he bumped the top of his little skull on the bottom of his little bed.

He was calling for help when he realized that he had fallen asleep in his ambush. He peered forth to see if he had snared Santa Claus.

The figure-4 trap was erect and intact, but empty. He crawled out and ran to the row of stockings he had hung on the mantelpiece as a decoy.

The stockings were empty.

With a shriek of disappointed rage, Ulie dashed into his parents' room to protest.

Their bed was empty.

He ran through the house, stumbled down stairs and into the back parlor. His father was snoring on a mattress of Yuletide parcels. His mother was curled up on a divan under the smoking piano lamp. Her hands were clutching strands of gold cord and her hair was pillowed in pink tissue paper. She was burbling in her sleep.

Little Ulie bent down to hear what she was saying. He made out faintly;

"Mishing you a Werry Muschris and a Nappy Hoosier."

The End